How to use this book

Follow the advice, in italics, given for you on each page.
Support the children as they read the text that is shaded in cream.
***Praise** the children at every step!*
Detailed guidance is provided in the Read Write Inc. Phonics Handbook.

9 reading activities
Children:
1 *Practise reading the speed sounds.*
2 *Read the green, red and challenge words for the non-fiction text.*
3 *Listen as you read the introduction.*
4 *Discuss the vocabulary check with you.*
5 *Read the non-fiction text.*
6 *Re-read the non-fiction text and discuss the 'questions to talk about'.*
7 *Re-read the non-fiction text with fluency and expression.*
8 *Answer the questions to 'read and answer'.*
9 *Practise reading the speed words.*

Speed sounds

Consonants *Say the pure sounds (do not add 'uh').*

f	l	m	n	r	s	v	z	sh	th	ng
ff	(ll)	mm	nn	rr	ss	ve	zz			nk
ph	le		kn	wr	(se)		se			
					(c)		s			
					ce					

b	c	d	g	h	j	p	qu	t	w	x	y	ch
bb	k	dd	gg		g	pp		(tt)	wh			(tch)
	ck				ge							

Vowels *Say the vowel sound and then the word, eg 'a', 'at'.*

at	hen	in	on	up	day	see	high	blow
	head				make	tea	smile	home
						happy	lie	no
						he	find	

zoo	look	car	for	fair	whirl	shout	boy
brute			door	care	nurse	cow	spoil
blue			snore		letter		
			yawn				

4 *Each box contains one sound but sometimes more than one grapheme. Focus graphemes are **circled**.*

Green words

Read in Fred Talk (pure sounds).

space   place   take   date   made   plane   same

shape   brave   high   side   like   life   light   ice

Moon   huge   found   first   air   Aldrin   distance   crater

diameter

Read in syllables.

a` bout  →  about    be` came → became   vis` it → visit

Arm` strong  →  Armstrong    A` poll` o → Apollo

De` cem` ber → December

Read the root word first and then with the ending.

high → high er   face → faces   shine → shines

reflect → reflected   patch → patches   orbit → orbits

Red words

any   do   d<u>oes</u>   o<u>th</u>er   <u>the</u>   <u>th</u>ere   <u>th</u>ey

was   wat<u>er</u>   w<u>ere</u>   <u>wh</u>at   <u>wh</u>o   to

Challenge words

ba<u>ll</u>   astron<u>au</u>ts   <u>Ear</u>th

humans   lun<u>ar</u>   alw<u>ay</u>s

A place in space: the Moon

Introduction

The Moon is a very long way from the Earth, but we can see light shining from it every night. Did you know that people called astronauts have landed on the Moon? Would you like to travel into space?

Written by Gill Munton

Vocabulary check

Discuss the meaning (as used in the non-fiction text) after the children have read the word.

	definition
formed	*made*
reflected light	*light shining back, like light from a mirror*
north, south	*different directions*
craters	*holes*
diameter	*distance across a ball shape*
lunar module	*small part of spacecraft in which astronauts can land*
orbits	*goes round*
poles	*top and bottom*
tides	*ebb and flow of sea to and from land*

Punctuation to note:

Up It Armstrong Moon	*Capital letters that start sentences and for names*
?	*Question mark at the end of each question*
–	*Hyphen before (and after) explanations or additional information*

What does the Moon look like?

Up in space, far higher than any plane can go, is the Moon.

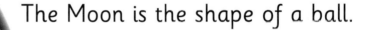

The Moon is the shape of a ball.

It has light patches – big hills – and dark patches – huge craters.

The craters were formed by space objects hitting the Moon at high speed.

What does the Moon do?

- The Moon orbits the Earth every 27.3 days.

  The same side always faces us, so we do not see the far side.

- It shines with reflected light from the Sun.

- It makes tides in the Earth's seas.

Moon

Earth

Moon fact

The Moon's diameter is about 3475 km.

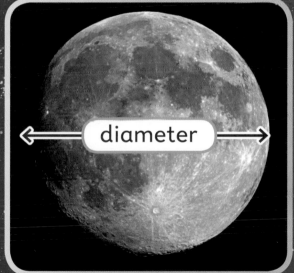

diameter

Is there life on the Moon?

air tank

There is no air on the Moon and there is no life. Astronauts who visit the Moon must take air with them in tanks.

An astronaut on the Moon

Moon fact

The Moon is about 384,400 km from Earth.

There is no air, but there is water – ice has been found at the north and south poles.

north pole

south pole

Who has landed on the Moon?

Brave astronauts have made visits to the Moon six times.

No other place in space has been landed on by humans.

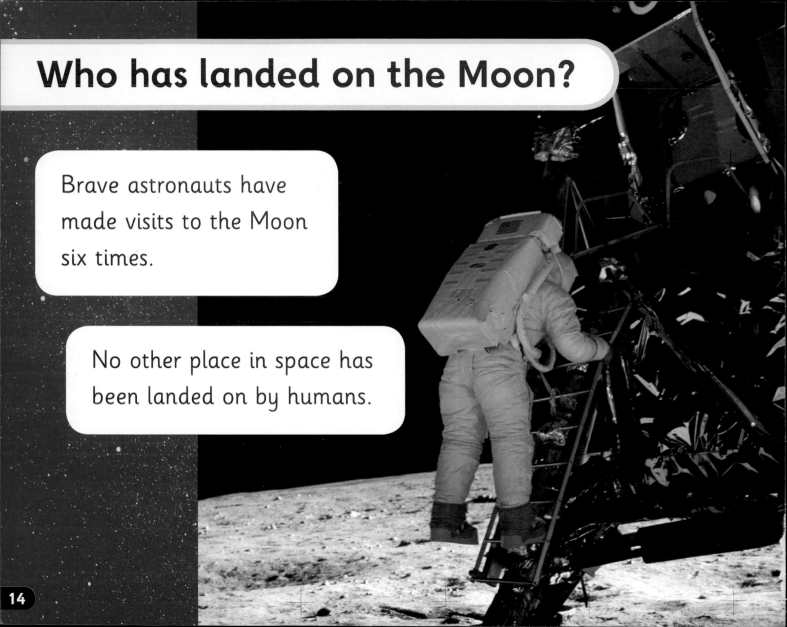

In 1969, American astronauts named Armstrong and Aldrin became the first humans to set foot on the Moon.

They landed in the lunar module of Apollo 11.

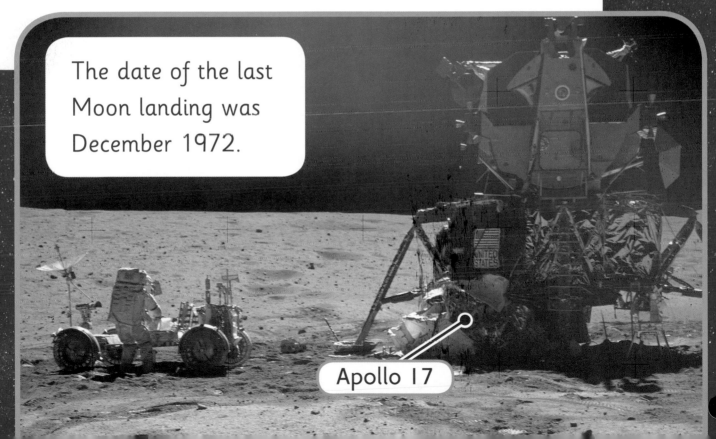

The date of the last Moon landing was December 1972.

Apollo 17

Who will be the next human to land on the Moon?

Questions to talk about

Re-read the page. Read the question to the children. Tell them whether it is a FIND IT question or PROVE IT question.

FIND IT	PROVE IT
✓ Turn to the page	✓ Turn to the page
✓ Read the question	✓ Read the question
✓ Find the answer	✓ Find your evidence
	✓ Explain why

Page 9:	FIND IT	*What made the craters on the Moon?*
Page 10:	FIND IT	*Why can't we see the far side of the Moon?*
Page 12:	PROVE IT	*Why do you think there is no life on the Moon?*
Page 13:	FIND IT	*Where has ice been found?*
Page 14:	PROVE IT	*Do you think it is safe to land on the Moon?*

Questions to read and answer

(Children complete without your help.)

1 What shape is the Moon?

2 What makes the tides in the sea?

3 What sort of water is on the Moon?

4 Who were the first men on the Moon?

5 When was the last Moon landing?